STORYFUN

4

STUDENT'S BOOK

with Online Activities
and Home Fun Booklet 4

Second edition

Karen Saxby

T0349655

Cambridge University Press
www.cambridge.org/elt

Cambridge Assessment English
www.cambridgeenglish.org

Information on this title: www.cambridge.org/9781316617175

© Cambridge University Press & Assessment 2017

First published 2011
Second edition 2017

40 39 38 37 36 35 34 33 32 31 30 29 28 27 26 25 24 23 22 21 20

Printed in India by Multivista Global Pvt Ltd

A catalogue record for this publication is available from the British Library

ISBN   978-1-316-61717-5   Student's Book with online activities and Home Fun booklet
ISBN   978-1-316-61719-9   Teacher's Book with Audio
ISBN   978-1-316-61723-6   Presentation Plus

Contents

Jane's clever idea

Jane lived in Fairfield. Everyone in the town knew her, but they never saw Jane walking. Jane loved her bike and loved riding to the shops and to school, but she loved riding her bike around the lake in the park most.

Last Friday, when Jane rode her bike between two park seats, a rabbit hopped out in front of her. She stopped really quickly and fell on the ground. Jane was OK because she always wore a helmet, but her bike wasn't. 'Oh no!' she thought. 'Now I need a new front wheel!'

'Mum!' she said, when she got home. 'Can you buy me a new front wheel for my bike?' 'Oh dear!' her mother answered. 'We need to buy a new swimsuit for your sister and a present for your grandmother. We can't buy you a new front wheel, too. Sorry, Jane.'

'But I need my bike to ride to school and the shops and around the lake, Mum!' Jane said.

'You can walk to school and the shops and go for nice walks in the park, Jane,' her mother answered.

Jane didn't like that idea. She went upstairs to her bedroom and thought and thought. Then she took a pair of ice skates from under her bed and went to find her friend, Sam.

'Sam!' she said. 'I need a new wheel for my bike. Have you got one? You can have these ice skates. Would you like them?'

'I'd like your ice skates,' Sam answered, 'but I haven't got a wheel for your bike. Would you like my tennis racket? I never play tennis now.'

'Well,' Jane said. 'I like your tennis racket more than these old ice skates. OK! Thanks.'

She gave Sam her ice skates and Sam gave Jane her tennis racket. Then Jane went to find her friend, Matt.

'Matt!' she said. 'I need a new wheel for my bike. Have you got one? You can have this tennis racket. Would you like it?'

'I'd like your tennis racket,' Matt answered, 'but I haven't got a wheel for your bike. Would you like these five CDs? The band's really cool, but all this music is on my new laptop now.'
'Well,' Jane said. 'I like those CDs more than this tennis racket. OK! Thanks.' She gave Matt the tennis racket and Matt gave Jane his five CDs. Then Jane went to find her friend, Paul.

'Paul!' she said. 'I need a new wheel for my bike. Have you got one? You can have these CDs. Would you like them?'
'I'd like your CDs,' Paul answered, 'but I haven't got a wheel for your bike. Would you like this old skateboard? It's too short and too slow for me.'

'Well,' Jane said. 'I like your skateboard more than these CDs. OK! Thanks.'
Jane gave Paul the CDs and Paul gave her his skateboard. Jane took it, stood on it and then rode back down the street on it. Jane's friend, Clare, was outside her house. She saw Jane and called, 'Hi! What a fantastic skateboard. Where did you get that?'

'Paul gave it to me,' Jane answered, 'He said it was too short and too slow for him. It's OK for me, but I don't really want it. I want a new wheel for my bike!'

'Well,' Clare said. 'My bike's very old, but both its wheels are fine. Would you like it?'
Jane started laughing. 'Yes, I would. I'd love it! Thanks!' she said. 'And would you like this skateboard?'
'Wow! Yes, please!' Clare said.
Jane gave Clare the skateboard and then rode Clare's old bike home.

Jane's mother was in the kitchen.
'You look happy,' she said.
'Well,' Jane said, 'I've got not one, but two new wheels for my bike!'
'What? How? Where from? When?' Jane's mother asked.
'I can't tell you now, Mum!' Jane laughed. 'I'm too busy.

I've got to fix my bike.

Then I want to ride around the lake six times before dinner!'

Jane's clever idea

A Read and draw lines.

1. This small animal has a round tail and hops!
2. Girls and women wear this when they swim.
3. People give these on birthdays.
4. This is on your head when you are riding a bike.
5. You can listen to music on these.
6. This means 'two' or 'two parts' of something.

a swimsuit
a pair
a helmet
presents
a rabbit
CDs

B Put the sentences in order.

a. Matt didn't want his CDs.
b. Sam gave Jane a tennis racket.
c. Jane's mum said 'Sorry.'
d. Paul gave Jane a skateboard.
e. Jane fixed her bike.
f. Clare talked to Jane.
g. Jane found some ice skates.
h. Jane saw a rabbit on the path.

C What might Jane say? Tick (✔) the correct answer.

A It is always exciting to try new hobbies. ☐

B Great friends always make you happy. ☐

C You don't always need to buy new things. ☐

D Read the text and choose the best answer.

Example

Ben: Hi Jane! Where are you going?

Jane: **A** Yes! This afternoon.
  B It's a different road.
  (C) Around the lake.

1 Ben: I love riding my bike here!

  Jane: **A** Fine thanks!
    B So do I!
    C Here you are!

2 Ben: Cool helmet! Is it new?

  Jane: **A** No, it was my cousin's.
    B No, there isn't one.
    C No, he's older than that.

3 Ben: Who gave you that bike?

  Jane: **A** My grandparents are here.
    B Miss Lily looks happy.
    C My uncle bought it for me.

4 Ben: And what's in your bag?

  Jane: **A** This map's not right.
    B Only a bottle of water.
    C It's on the seat.

5 Ben: Do you like those ducks?

  Jane: **A** I like penguins more.
    B Let's go swimming.
    C Yes, please. Thanks!

E What do you like? Look and say with *more* and *the most*.

I like snails, but I like bees more.

I like butterflies the most.

9

F **03** Mr Pool is telling Jane about the people in his family. What does each person really like doing? Listen and write a letter in each box.

grandson   cousin   daughter   granddaughter   son   father

   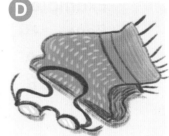

  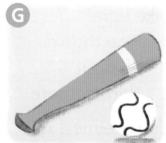 

G Read and draw lines.

1 I'd like a tree house.   Well, let's wash them!

2 This music is boring.   Well, we can play in my room!

3 There's no lemonade!   Well, let's find a website!

4 It's raining outside.   Well, we can make some!

5 I'd like to learn about bears.   Well, let's sing a song!

6 My football boots are too dirty.   Well, we can build one!

H Find five differences. Point and say.

Here, the ducks are in the water.

But here, they're on the grass.

I **04** Listen and sing. Then change the coloured words.

I do like
to ride my bike…
up that field .... ,
on the farm .... and
around the funfair .... ,
behind the zoo .... and
along the beach .... ,
opposite the car park ....
and near the river .... ,
in the forest .... and
down Duck Road ....
Oh! And on the moon ....
But never, never
inside our house .... !

p 68

p 72

11

The perfect present

2

Jim's favourite teacher was called Miss Point. Miss Point helped Jim learn lots of different things. She taught him about words and work and earache and emails and ships and shapes. She was never angry when Jim made spelling mistakes and she played basketball with Jim and his classmates in their morning break. Miss Point was great and Jim wanted to give her a present. But he had no ideas.

Jim went for a walk along the river and then sat down to think. He watched the water. He watched a frog that jumped off an old boat and caught three fat flies in the river plants. He watched a lizard that slept on a rock. He watched two bees that buzzed in circles above some ducks. It's so beautiful here. Jim said.

Mr and Mrs Star and their daughter, Grace, liked walking by the river, too. They stopped when they saw Jim. 'Hi, Jim. Are you all right?' Mrs Star asked.

'Hello, Mrs Star,' Jim answered. 'I want to give my teacher a present. But it's difficult. Can you help me choose one?'

'We can try,' said Grace. 'What does your teacher like?'

'She likes the internet and trips on the train and she loves weekends,' answered Jim. 'But I can't give her those.'

'No,' said Mr Star. 'You can't! What colour does she like?'

'She likes green,' Jim said. 'She painted our bookcase green. I'd like to give her a green apple tree or the prettiest green parrot in the world, but I can't do that.'

'No, you can't,' said Grace. 'Apple trees look nicer when they're growing in a field and parrots look prettier when they're flying in the forest!'

'How about a lime or some peas or beans?' asked Mrs Star.
'They're green.'

'No,' said Jim. 'I don't want to give her any of those things.'

'Then a salad?' asked Grace.

'Yes!' said Jim, 'She likes salad! My aunt grows salad leaves in her garden. I can take her some of those ... But that's not enough.'

'Well, does she like the colour blue?' asked Mr Star.

'Yes,' said Jim. 'She painted our classroom door blue! I'd like to give her the beautiful blue sea or five hundred blue flowers, but I can't give her those.'

'No, you can't,' said Grace. 'The sea looks nicer next to white sand, and blue flowers look more beautiful when they're growing in the green grass!'

'What about a blue bowl or pen or a blue watch?' asked Mrs Star.

'No,' said Jim. 'I don't want to give her any of those things.'

'How about some blue grapes, then?' asked Grace.

'Oh! She loves grapes! That's a fantastic idea!' Jim said. 'And we grow grapes in our garden. I can take her some of those ... But that's not enough.'

'Does she like yellow?' Mr Star asked.

'Yes!' answered Jim. 'Yellow's her favourite. Our classroom clock is yellow. I'd like to give her the sun or a yellow butterfly, but I can't give her those.'

'No,' said Grace. 'You can't. The sun looks more beautiful above the mountains and yellow butterflies look prettier when they're flying in the sky.'

'What about a yellow apple, some lemons or a banana?' asked Mrs Star.

'No,' said Jim. 'I don't want to give her any of those things.'

'Cheese is yellow,' Grace said.

'Yes! Yes! She likes cheese! That's a brilliant idea! We make cheese at home from my favourite cow's milk,' said Jim. 'I know my teacher loves the internet and train trips and weekends, but she LOVES picnics, too. And green salad leaves, blue grapes and yellow cheese are great things to take on a picnic. I can give her those. Thank you for helping me choose a perfect present for Miss Point!'

Jim and the Star family jumped up and walked slowly home.
The frog jumped up, too, and ate another fat fly.

2 The perfect present

A Read and complete the words.

1. A t r i p on a train to the countryside is so exciting!
2. I'm reading about lizards on the **in _ _ _ _ _ t**.
3. Can we play basketball in the playground in our **b _ _ _ k?**
4. I made a **m _ _ _ _ ke** in my spelling when I wrote 'butterfly'.
5. We took some cheese sandwiches to eat on our **p _ _ _ _ c!**
6. I don't send my classmates **e _ _ _ ls**. I send them texts.

B Read and circle the correct answer.

1. The frog that Jim watched ate some **snails / (flies)**.
2. Grace was Mr and Mrs Star's **daughter / granddaughter**.
3. Grace thought apple trees looked nicer in a **field / forest**.
4. Jim's **uncle / aunt** grows salad leaves in the garden.
5. Jim wants to give his teacher some blue **grapes / plants**.
6. Grace said the **moon / sun** looks beautiful above the mountains.

C Look at the picture on page 12 and talk with a friend.

| beautiful **brilliant** sunny |
| nice quiet pretty *funny* |
| fantastic *cool* |

Wow! The .... is beautiful!

D Read and draw lines.

1. Here's the present **that**
2. This is the mountain **that**
3. There's the frog **that**
4. These are the plants **that**
5. This is the walk **that**
6. Those are the bees **that**

ate three fat flies.

Jim chose for his teacher.

we went on last weekend.

talks like a parrot.

we grow in our field.

Jim's parents climbed.

flew above our blue flowers.

E Look and read. Choose the correct words and write them on the lines.

a parrot

cheese

the alphabet

a salad

a snail

a website

homework

a picnic

Example

You look for and find this on the internet. .....a website.....

Questions

1. You can make this with vegetables that you don't cook. ....
2. This animal moves slowly and has a shell on its back. ....
3. This is food that you take to eat outside. ....
4. Your teacher gives you this and you do it at home. ....
5. Sometimes you can teach this clever animal to talk. ....

F Read the text and then write one from you.

Hi! We're having fun. This place is fantastic! This morning, we went fishing. We saw some parrots! The weather here is cloudy. But that's OK. See you on Saturday. Bye :)

Hello! We're having fun, too! It's **1** ......*brilliant*...... here.
Yesterday, we **2** .... We saw some
3 .... The weather's **4** ....
But I'm **5** .... See you on **6** ....
Bye!

G Look at the pictures. Tell the story.

The picnic and the parrot

This is Julia and Peter. They are going for a walk.

1

2

3

4

H ▶ 06 Listen and colour the picture on page 13.

I ▶ 07 Listen and sing the song.

How I do like to sit here on the grass.
Here on the grass so green.
Oh, I do think it's the very best place
    any child or grown-up can see.

How I do like to look up at the sky.
Up at the sky so blue.
Oh, I do think it's the very best thing
    any child or grown-up can do.

How I do like to play here in the sun.
Play here in the sun so gold.
Oh, I do think it's the very best place,
    the very best place in the world.

p 68

p 72

19

Daisy's tiger dream

3

Daisy had a beautiful, big bedroom with big windows and a big balcony. She had lots of nice clothes to wear, different computer games to play, music to listen to and movies to watch. She had fantastic roller skates, a new guitar and hundreds of books, comics, paints and crayons.

'Oh! But I'm not happy,' she thought one night when she went to bed. 'I know! I can ask my parents to buy me some more exciting games and … and a longer skateboard, a better bike and a newer laptop. Yes, that's a great idea!' Then Daisy went to sleep and had a very strange dream.

In her dream, Daisy saw a lake and a big mountain. She couldn't see the top of the mountain and Daisy couldn't hear any birds or any animals. She could only hear the wind.

There was a little white boat on the lake. Daisy got into it and, in the light of the moon and stars, the boat sailed quietly across the water to a cave.

When the boat stopped, Daisy got out and looked into the cave. She saw some steps and went down, down, down into the mountain. She counted the steps: 44, 45 … 61, 62 … 97, 98, 99, 100! When she stood on the last step, Daisy saw a small orange light in front of her.

The orange light got bigger and bigger.
'It's a tiger!' she thought, 'and it's coming nearer and nearer, but I'm OK. I'm brave. I'm not frightened.'
The tiger opened its mouth.
'I'm NOT frightened,' Daisy thought again.

'Ask me a question, child,' the tiger said quietly.

'Why aren't I the happiest child in the world? I have really cool clothes and lots of exciting games and brilliant CDs and movies.'

'People aren't happy because they have *things*, child,' the tiger said. 'Be a good friend and be kind to animals and enjoy the light from the sun, moon and stars. Do that and you can be happy again.'

Then Daisy woke up. She heard her phone. Her friends never called her before breakfast!

'Hi, Daisy. It's Jack here. You and I never talk at school, because you're always too busy, but I can't do our music homework. You're very good at music. Can you help me with that? I've got a new guitar too. I know you're very good at playing the guitar.
Can you ... can you help me learn to play the guitar too?'
Daisy thought about her dream. She smiled and said, 'Yes, Jack. I can help you do your homework and give you guitar lessons!'

'You're really kind,' Jack said. 'Thanks a lot!'

Daisy went downstairs to have her breakfast.

Her mum was in the kitchen. 'Daisy,' she said, 'we've got something for you.'

'But I don't want a better bike or a ...' Daisy started to say.
Her mum pointed to a black and orange kitten and said, 'Dad found it outside last night. Be kind to it. It needs a good friend!'

Daisy thought about her dream again. She picked the kitten up and smiled at it. 'Hello!' she said. 'What a pretty face! You look like a tiger that I know! But you're smaller and more beautiful.'
'What tiger?' Daisy's mum asked. But Daisy didn't answer.

'I'm really happy this morning, Mum,' she said. I can be a good friend.

'I can help Jack do his homework and learn the guitar. I can be kind to this funny little kitten – and look at the sun!
It's a beautiful sunny day outside. Wow! What a great day!'

3

 # Daisy's tiger dream

 **A** Read and write the correct word.

~~stars~~ busy **outside** sailed ~~dream~~ pretty

1 Daisy had a strange ...*dream*... that night.

2 There were hundreds of .... in the sky above the lake.

3 Daisy .... to the cave in a little white boat.

4 Jack says Daisy is always .... when she's at school.

5 The kitten was .... the house when Dad found it.

6 The orange and black kitten had a .... face.

 B Draw lines and make sentences.

1 Daisy wanted to   Daisy a kitten.
2 In her dream, Daisy   Jack phoned her.
3 The tiger spoke to   be happier.
4 Daisy woke up when   saw a sailing boat.
5 Daisy's mother gave   bottom of the steps.
6 Daisy met a tiger at the   Daisy very slowly.

 C Who's talking about this story? Listen and tick (✔) the box.

09

A
Hi! My name's Alice.

B
Hello! My name's Ben.

C
I'm Jim.

☐   ☐   ☐

D Complete the sentences with *-er* or *more*.

1 Daisy's room was (small) ....smaller........ than her friend's room.

2 Daisy's dress was (beautiful) ..more beautiful.. than her friend's dress.

3 Daisy's TV was (new) .... than Sally's TV.

4 Daisy's games were (boring) .... than Paul's games.

5 Daisy's guitar was (loud) .... than Jack's guitar.

6 Daisy's homework was (difficult) .... than Ben's homework.

7 Daisy's kitten was (young) .... than Lily's cat.

E Complete the sentences.

1 Daisy asked ...her mum.... to buy her a new ......guitar...... . She said yes! ☺

2 Jack asked .....his dad.... to buy him a new .....jacket...... . He said no! ☹

3 I asked .... to buy me a new .... said .... ! ◯

4 I asked .... to give me a .... said .... ! ◯

5 I asked .... to give me a .... said .... ! ◯

F Read the text. Choose the right words and write them on the lines.

① I ......*had*........ a great day today. I went to Jack's house after school because he	had	has	having
② asked me .... help him with his	for	to	after
③ homework. Then we played	ours	us	our
④ guitars. His guitar is .... than mine. We played very loudly! I'm not	new	newer	newest
⑤ good .... singing, but Jack is. We	in	on	at
⑥ had lots .... fun and laughed a lot too. I thought about my tiger dream	of	from	off
⑦ again after dinner. I don't .... a nicer bike or a longer skateboard. I know that now!	needs	needing	need

G Which one is different? Look and say.

> The boat! The boat is green but the tomato, skateboard and pencil are red.

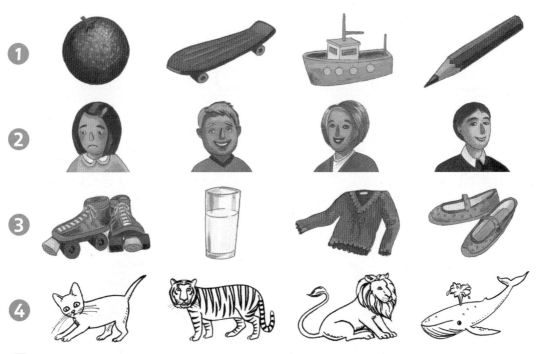

▶ Look at the animals. Listen and colour.

10

H Listen and write.
11

Daisy's kitten

    Name: ....*Tiger*...........

1   Enjoys playing with: Daisy's old ....

2   Is good at: ....

3   Likes eating: ....

4   Sleeps: on a ....

5   Understands which word: ....

I Let's talk about friends. Ask and answer questions with a friend.

> What do you enjoy doing with your friends?

> Where do you and your friends like going?

> When do you phone or text your friends?

> Tell me about your best friend.

p 69

p 72

A busy Monday

The snow started falling on Friday night. It snowed all weekend too. On Monday morning, everything outside was white. 'It's not safe to drive today,' a man on the radio said. 'All the schools are closed. And the roads are too dangerous to go to the sports centre or to go to the circus this evening, everyone. Sorry!'

 My mum and dad picked up their phones. Mum called the place where she works. She's a dentist. And Dad called the café where he works. He's a cook.

'No work today!' they said.

Mum said I must clean the hall rug. 'And water all the plants, too. Let's have a busy day at home. I can make a meat and potato pie, then I'd like to paint the hall.'

'Well,' said Dad. 'I must fix the washing machine, then I'd like to make some bread and some onion soup and then read my new e-book. Mark, you must clean your pet rabbit's cage, feed the puppy and practise the piano. And how about making that model spaceship?'

'All right,' I said. 'But some pieces are missing, I think. ... Oh! I've got a text from Alex.'

Alex is my best friend. I read his message and sent him a quick answer.

Alex helped me clean the rabbit's cage. That wasn't easy and we had to catch the rabbit! We didn't feed the puppy because it was asleep on one of Dad's sweaters and we didn't want to wake it up. We practised on the piano. We aren't very good, but we had fun!

Then we looked at the instructions to make the model spaceship. 'There are 57 pieces ...' I said, 'and we must start with these four little ones.'
Alex counted the pieces. 'There are only 53,' he said. 'Those four little ones aren't here.'
'We haven't got all the pieces for the spaceship!' I called to my parents.
'Well, help me paint this hall!' Mum said.
'Or help me fix this washing machine!' Dad said.
'Or play your new computer game!' Alex said quietly.
I laughed. 'Great idea!' I said.

It's not the best computer game that I've got, but it's funny. Alex and I laughed a lot. We had to make the animals move really quickly to catch boats, trains or buses or ride in trucks or fly in helicopters.

At the end of the game, the kangaroo was in the supermarket, the lion was in the library, the zebra was in the cinema and the panda was at the funfair.

'Good game?' asked Dad.

'It was OK,' we answered.

'Lunch?' asked Mum.

'Fantastic!' we answered.

After lunch, Mum made a scarf and emailed all her old school friends. Dad cleaned his football boots and tidied the basement. Alex and I fed our sweet, little puppy, which was awake. Then we taught my parrot to say 'Busy Day! Busy Day!' Dad videoed it! 'Well!' Dad said. 'It WAS a busy day!'

'Yes,' I said. 'I like being busy. Alex and I cleaned the rabbit's cage, did some piano practice, took a kangaroo from a car park to the supermarket and a lion to the library, drove a zebra to the cinema and flew a panda to the funfair, fed the puppy, and taught our parrot to say 'Busy Day!'

'That's right, but what about making that model spaceship?' Dad asked.
'We couldn't find the last four pieces!' Alex said.

'Do you mean these?' Dad asked.
'I found them in the washing machine!'

'YES!' I said. 'HOORAY!'

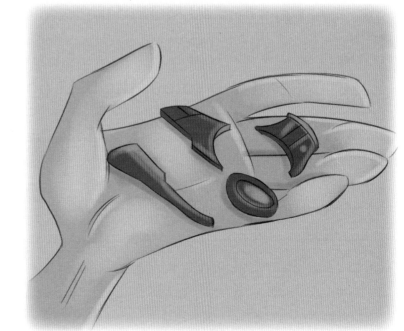

A busy Monday

4

A Read and write the correct number.

1. This person fixes teeth!
2. When you are dreaming, you are this.
3. This has lots of parts which move.
4. This means to film something.
5. This person is good at making dinner!
6. You are not sleeping when you are this!

asleep ☐
dentist ☐ 1
to video ☐
awake ☐
cook ☐
machine ☐

B Read and answer the questions.

1. Which day was Mark's busy day? ....Monday....
2. What couldn't the boys make? a model ....
3. Which part of the house did Mum paint? the ....
4. What kind of soup did Dad make? .... soup
5. Which part of the house did Dad tidy? the ....
6. What did Mum make to wear? a ....

C Read and colour the best answer green.

I like being busy!

A Yes, I think it is!

B What are they like?

C Brilliant! So do I!

D What must you do this week? Write five things.

1 I must ....

....

....

E Read the story. Choose a word from the box. Write the correct word next to numbers 1–5.

Mark wants to be a cook one day. Last weekend, he said to his ....*parents*...... , 'I'd like to make lunch!'

'OK!' said Dad. 'Well, I must go into the garden and plant some **1** ....'

'All right.' said Mum. 'Well I must go upstairs and clean the bathroom **2** ....'

Mark washed and dried his hands. He cooked some noodles and made some tomato sauce. Then he read a text from Alex.

Mark's cousin, Julia, called to tell him about the fantastic goal she **3** .... in her hockey game! He played a difficult word game on his phone. Then Alex sent him another **4** .... which he answered.

'How's our lunch?' Dad called from the garden.

'Yes! How's our lunch?' Mum called from upstairs.

'Oh dear! Sorry.' Mark said. 'The noodles and sauce aren't **5** .... now.'

'Don't worry!' laughed Dad. 'I'm coming to help.'

Example

parents	floor	hot	hid	terrible

message	scored	vegetables	square

---

6 Now choose the best name for the story. Tick (✔) one box.

Mark plays hockey ☐   Mark's new game ☐   Mark makes lunch ☐

F 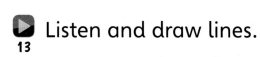 Listen and draw lines.

13

1

2

3

café

cinema

car park

pool

library

market

4

5

6

G Listen and tick (✔) the box.

14

Example

What does Jack want for lunch?

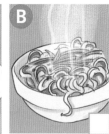 **A** 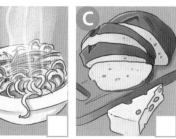 **B**  **C**

1 Who is Julia sending a text to?

A  **B**  **C**

2 What is Mum doing now?

A 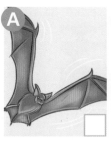 **B**  **C**

3 What is in Charlie's video?

4 Where is Grandpa this afternoon?

A  **B** 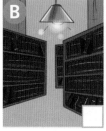 **C**

5 What is Dad fixing now?

A  **B** 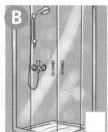 **C**

Look at the picture. Complete the sentences and answer the questions.

On the wall, there is a ....*mirror*.............. .

What is the man carrying? .*two cups of coffee*.

1. In the street, someone is riding a ....

2. The man is wearing a ....

3. Who is sitting at the round table? ....

4. What can you buy in this café? ....

▶ Listen and say the poem.

15

Dad's driving me to school.
Oh! There's the swimming pool.
On the road, there's snow.
Go slow, Dad. Go slow!

Here's the centre of our town.
Dad looks up, round and down.
On the Square, there's more snow!
It is dangerous, I know!

We're at my school now.
I can see my friends, but 'Oh!
There's no snow here,' I call.
'That's no fun at all!'

p 69

p 72

The tomango tree

Tom lived on a farm. Behind the farm, there was a big forest on a hill. Tom liked walking there and climbing the trees where the forest birds sang and sang. There was a river near the farm where Tom often fished, too. He loved living in the countryside.

Tom's parents both worked on the farm. They fed their cows, sheep, goats and chickens and planted vegetables in their fields.

'I'd like to grow fruit here too,' his father often said. He tried to grow pears, but they were too small. He couldn't grow bananas. They were always too green. And the weather was too cold to grow kiwis, watermelons or pineapples.
'Find a fruit we can grow here, Tom,' his father said.

One morning, Tom woke up and walked to his window. The river looked like a mirror in the sun and the trees danced in the wind.
'Hmm,' Tom thought. 'Today is a good day to be in the forest.'

After breakfast, he put some water in his bag and started to walk up the hill. Up and up he went. At the top of the hill, Tom sat down under the tallest tree. 'This tree is really tall!' he thought. 'I want to climb it! Yes! Now!'

Up and up he climbed. From the top of the tree, Tom could see more hills, his family's farm buildings, their home, their truck and tractor and all of their fields. He could see the river and the sea, too.

One day, I want to climb all those hills.

Tom thought, 'I want to work on the farm and grow fruit. But I want to sail down that river and across the sea, too. One day, I want to go to countries where there are mountains, waterfalls and jungles. I want to do hundreds and hundreds of exciting things.'

Suddenly, Tom heard something. It was in the tree below him, but it wasn't a bird. 'It's a fruit bat – the kind of bat that only eats fruit,' thought Tom. 'Cool! I'm lucky to find one of those!'

Tom heard the fruit bat again, but he couldn't see it. He started to climb down the tree and saw something red behind a big leaf. It moved. 'A red fruit bat?' thought Tom. 'That's very strange!'

Tom moved the leaf, but the red thing wasn't an animal.
It was like a kind of tomato or mango. And there wasn't only one.
There were lots and lots of them.
Tom picked one of the strange fruits and looked at it more carefully.
Then he ate it. It was really good! Tom was hungry!
He ate another one and another one.
Then he picked five more and put them in his bag.

'I must give this fruit a name,' he thought. 'I know. It's a tomango!'

Tom climbed back down the tree and he ran home to show the fruit to his father.

'Look, Dad!' he called. 'I found a tomango tree in the forest. We can grow *this* fruit here on our farm.'

And they did. Tom's father took the five tomangoes and grew plants from them. Soon the family had hundreds of small tomango trees, and people came from the city to buy all the wonderful fruit that grew on them.

But there's a strange end to this story. When he was older, Tom did lots of exciting things. He sailed down the river and across the sea. He climbed hills and mountains in different countries, and sometimes he came home and climbed trees again, too. But Tom never, never, found another tomango tree or heard a fruit bat in the forest above the farm again.

5 The tomango tree

A Write the words (2–9) in the correct box.

Look for this in the city!

Look for this in the countryside!

> 1 a big forest

> **1** a big forest **2** a tall building **3** a beautiful waterfall
> **4** a bus stop **5** a green field **6** a little farm
> **7** a shopping centre **8** an old tractor **9** a busy street

B Put the sentences in order.

Tom climbed the tallest tree in the forest. | 1

Tom saw some strange red fruit.

Tom ate the strange fruit.

Tom heard a fruit bat in the tree.

Tom's father planted the fruit.

Tom gave the fruit to his father.

Tom put some fruit in his bag.

C Read and write *right* or *wrong*.

1 Tom found a red bird in a tall tree. ......wrong......

2 Tom's parents were teachers. ....

3 The forest was behind Tom's farm. ....

4 Tom often went fishing in the river. ....

5 Tom only took one tomango home. ....

6 When he was older Tom went to some exciting places. ....

D What do you want to do one day? Tell a friend and write.

One day, I want to ....
....
and ....
....
and ....
....

One day, I want to sail across the sea!

E Look, read and write *A* or *B*.

1 Tom could see the river. ....A....

2 Tom couldn't see the farm. ....

3 Tom could carry lots of things in his bag. ....

4 Tom couldn't hear the bird's song. ....

5 Tom could see more than three small trees. ....

6 Tom couldn't take any photos. ....

F ▶ Find the picture on page 36. Listen, colour and write.
17

G Complete the sentences with a word from the box.

eat   sing   grow   put   ~~take~~

1. Julia ....*took*........ a book to the forest.
2. Julia .... a pretty plant on the grass.
3. A bird .... a song.
4. Fruit .... in the green tree.
5. Julia .... a tomango!

H ▶ Listen and draw lines.
18

Paul   Clare   Fred   Jane

Vicky   Charlie   Sally

I Find and write the words.

treeshatstravellingcakesCDsplaying

Tom loves climbing very tall **1** ....trees......... .
I love kicking old brown leaves.
Tom likes swimming in cold lakes.
I like eating coffee **2** ....
Tom loves fishing in the rain.
I love **3** .... on the train.
Tom likes playing his **4** ....
I like watching DVDs!
Tom loves looking for fruit bats.
And I love wearing funny **5** .... !
Tom likes helping his vegetables to grow.
And I like **6** .... in the snow!

J Let's talk about free time. Ask and answer questions with friends. Complete the table.

What do you like doing after school?

Who do you play games with?

Where do you play games?

Tell me about your favourite hobby.

p 70

p 73

	Me:	Friend 1:	Friend 2: ....
What / like doing?			
Who / play with?			
Where / play?			

Do whales have stomach-ache?

My younger brother is called Fred. Fred's very interested in animals. He talks and asks questions about animals *all* the time. Fred's really interested in parrots, pandas, polar bears and penguins and lions and leopards and rabbits. But Fred's favourite animals live in the sea. He has posters of jellyfish, whales, dolphins, sharks and octopuses on all the walls of his bedroom.

Look at my picture, Mum. This is an octopus. Why do octopuses have eight arms?

Or are they legs? Why are there little cups on their arms?

Fred doesn't stop talking when I'm doing my homework or when Mum's trying to read quietly.

'Sssssssssshhhh, Fred!' we have to say sometimes.

Last Saturday, Fred wanted to go to the library in town to get a book called *The Most Dangerous Animals in the World*. He wanted to get a DVD called *Leopard's Spots*, too.

But Mum said, 'No, Fred. You don't look well. I want Aunt Jane to come and see you. You've got lots of little red spots on your face.'

Aunt Jane is a doctor. She knows all about red spots!

Fred looked in the mirror. 'But I'm not ill and my spots aren't scary and they don't hurt,' he said.

Do you know, Mum, leopards have spots, and there's a kind of dog called a Dalmatian that has hundreds of spots too**?**

'Yes, I know!' Mum said.

When Aunt Jane saw Fred, she asked 'Have you got any spots on your body? On your back, your shoulders or arms?'

'No,' Fred said. 'Octopuses have got eight arms. Did you know that, Aunt Jane? They've got three hearts too!'

'Have they?' Aunt Jane said. 'Can I look in your ears now?'

'And do you know, Aunt Jane? A blue whale is the biggest animal in the world!' Fred said.

'Yes, Fred,' Aunt Jane answered. 'But can I look in your eyes now? That's right. Look up! Good … and down!'

'And dolphins are the cleverest animals in the sea,' Fred said.

'Mmm,' Aunt Jane said.
'Have you got a cold or a cough?'

'No,' Fred answered and started talking again. 'Sharks are the most dangerous kind of fish. When a shark loses a tooth, they can't go to the dentist. But it's OK! Another tooth grows! Do you think sharks have toothache sometimes?'

'Fred, stop talking, please. I want to look in your mouth now! Say AAAAAHHHHH!'

'AAAAAHHHHH!' Fred said, and then started talking again!

'And dolphins are good at bouncing balls on their heads. Do you think they have headaches sometimes?'
'I don't know, Fred,' Aunt Jane said.

Then she smiled at him and said, 'Well, you haven't got a temperature, but you need some medicine and you mustn't go shopping today. You can go to the shopping centre to get your book and DVD on Monday. OK?'

Aunt Jane opened a bottle of green medicine and put some
on a spoon. Fred didn't like medicine.
He stopped talking because he didn't want to open his mouth.

'You must open your mouth now, please,
Fred,' Aunt Jane said.
But Fred didn't open his mouth.

Aunt Jane had a clever idea.

'Do you think whales have stomach-ache
sometimes, Fred?' she asked.

Fred started to say, 'I—'

When Fred did that, Aunt Jane quickly put the medicine into his open
mouth!

'That's horrible!' Fred said, but then he smiled. 'Hey! I like this medicine
a lot. It's the nicest medicine in the world. Can I have some more?'

Aunt Jane laughed. 'No!' she said.

'You can have a glass of orange juice,' Mum said.

But then Fred started talking again. 'Whales don't drink orange juice,
but they do have stomach-ache, I think. They have *very* big stomachs.
Do you know they eat—'

'Sssssssssshhhh, Fred!' I said.
'Sssssssssshhhh, Fred!' Mum said and
'Sssssssssshhhh, Fred!' Aunt Jane said.

6 Do whales have stomach-ache?

A Read and write the correct word.

a panda   a dentist   ~~a bottle~~   a cup   a rabbit   a doctor   a lion

1 People can sometimes buy fruit juice in this.   ...*a bottle*...

2 This kind of bear is black and white.   ....

3 This animal has a small round tail and hops.   ....

4 People who are ill go and see this person.   ....

5 This big animal eats meat and is sometimes scary!   ....

6 This person is good at fixing teeth.   ....

B Put the sentences (2–9) in the correct box.

1 Fred liked being quiet.   **2** Fred had spots on his face.

3 Fred's aunt came to see him.   **4** Fred's aunt was a dentist.

5 Fred looked in his aunt's ears.   **6** Fred had a really bad cold.

7 Fred's medicine was green.   **8** Fred got his DVD on Saturday.

9 Fred thinks whales have stomach-ache!

right   **wrong**

1

C. What's different? Circle the wrong words. Write the right words.

Did you know that ...?

asks

Fred talks and (answers) questions about animals all the time. Fred is really interested in parents, pancakes, polar bears and penguins and libraries and leopards and rainbows. But Fred's favourite apartments live in the sky. He has posters of jellyfish, whales, dolls, showers and octopuses on all the walls of his basement.

D. Talk with a friend and complete the sentences.

beautiful	small	**tall**	scary	dangerous	clever	**slow**
ugly	interesting	strong	loud	silly	big	short

1 I think blue whales are ....*the biggest*........ animals in the sea.

2 My friend thinks kangaroos are *the most interesting* animals in the world.

3 I think bears are .... animals in the world.

Dolphins are the cleverest animals in the sea.

4 My friend thinks pandas are .... animals in the world.

5 I think sharks are .... kind of fish.

6 My friend thinks penguins are .... animals at our zoo.

7 I think snails are .... animals in our park.

E ▶ Listen and tick (✔) the box.
20

1 Where are Fred's spots?

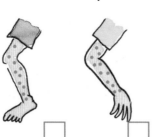

☐   ☐   ☐

2 What hurts?

☐   ☐   ☐

3 What's the matter with Fred now?

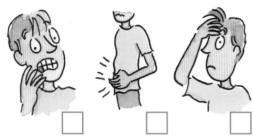

☐   ☐   ☐

4 Why isn't Fred at school today?

☐   ☐   ☐

F Read and draw lines to make sentences.

1 Fred went to the library to   buy some medicine.

2 Fred's dad drove to the shop to   look at his spots.

3 Aunt Jane came to see Fred to   get a new book.

4 Fred's mum phoned Aunt Jane to   ask her to come.

5 Fred's classmate emailed Fred to   practise skateboarding.

6 Fred's brother went to the park to   ask about his English lesson.

G Let's talk about Fred's brother. Ask and answer with a friend. Complete the notes.

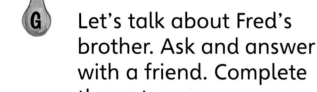

How old is he?

What does he like eating?

What's his first name?

Which sports does he enjoy doing?

First name: ....

Family name: ....

Age: ....

Address: ....

How he travels to school: ....

....

Likes eating: ....

Sports: ....

H Find six differences. Point and say.

> In this picture, there's a whale on the poster. But in this picture, it's a dolphin.

1

2

I Look at picture 2 in H. Read and write.

Examples

The boy in the jeans is standing on a pink ......*chair*...... .
Which animal is running on the grass? ......*a dog*...... .

Complete the sentences.

1 There is a computer on the ....

2 The woman at the grey table is wearing ....

Answer the questions.

3 What is the girl in the armchair doing? ....

4 Which animal is in the poster? ....

Now write two sentences about the picture.

5 ....

6 ....

p 70
p 73

The grey cloud

7

I was on a long, boring train ride with my aunt. I looked out of the window at the rain. The countryside looked grey and cold.

'Tell me a story, Aunt Clare,' I said. 'One about the rain.'
'All right,' she said. This is the story she told me.

'There was a small cloud in the sky above the apartment where Lily lived. Sometimes the cloud got angry because the wind was too strong, or because it was alone in the sky.

When the cloud got really angry, it got slowly bigger and greyer. Its grey colour fell on to the roof of Lily's apartment building. It also fell into Lily's roof garden and when Lily went outside to skip, she couldn't see the red and yellow flowers there. She could only see grey ones. Lily often got angry then, too.

Sometimes the cloud wasn't only angry. It got really sad. When the cloud felt really angry AND sad, it felt worse and it cried and its wet rain fell on Lily's windows and balcony.
Lily didn't like being wet. She couldn't go outside and dance on the garden table because she didn't like getting her head, neck and shoulders wet. Lily often got angry AND sad then, too.

Sometimes the cloud wasn't only angry and sad. It often got frightened. When the cloud felt frightened, it felt colder. Then its snow fell quietly on the ground and rocks and on the mountains behind Lily's home, and water changed to ice. Walking in the snow and on the ice was difficult and dangerous. Lily often got angry, sad and frightened then too.

Monday wasn't a good day. The cloud was huge and very grey.

Lily couldn't see any light from the sun.

She couldn't see her feet on the ground.

And, at night, Lily couldn't see any light from the moon or stars.

Tuesday and Wednesday were worse. Nothing was different. On Thursday morning, when Lily got up and saw no light outside again, she thought, 'I've got to do something about this!' She climbed up the stairs to the roof garden.

'Cloud!' Lily called from the top of the roof. 'This is the worst day of my week! I love looking at you when you are small and white, and when you skip and dance and climb in the wind. But why are you huge and so grey now? What IS the matter?'

The cloud started to cry.

'The wind is strong and I am weak and I have no friends,' cried the cloud. 'That makes me angry and sad, and I get bigger and greyer. I feel worse and worse and then my rain falls.'

'Oh dear!' said Lily.

'And sometimes I get frightened because I have no friends. When I feel frightened, I get really cold and my snow falls,' added the cloud. 'Well, shall I be your best friend today? I know I can make you feel better again. Stronger too!' Lily said to the cloud and started to skip along the roof garden. 'And when you feel happy again, I can be happier, too!' she said.

'Come on! Let's skip!' Lily took off her coat and started to skip around the grey flowers and the cloud slowly started to skip around the sun.

'That's better, but more quickly! More quickly!' laughed Lily. 'Come on, my friend! Now, let's dance!' Lily jumped up onto the table, waved her arms around and started to dance and the cloud slowly started to dance in the wind.

'Fantastic!' laughed Lily. 'Now, Come on! Are you feeling better or worse?'

'Better!' said the cloud.

'Great! Then now, let's climb!' Lily started to climb her favourite rock and the cloud started to climb in the sky. 'Higher, higher!' Lily called.

And when the cloud skipped and danced and climbed with Lily, its colour changed from grey to white and a beautiful rainbow appeared in the sky. The cloud was happy again and Lily couldn't stop laughing.

That's better!

But it wasn't always like that.

On some days of the year, the cloud's rain and snow fell because it felt angry or sad or frightened again. Lily understood that.

'We can't always feel happy,' Aunt Clare said. 'But skipping, dancing and climbing and laughing and playing with really good friends can always help us feel better again. Now pick up your bag! Here's our station!'

7 **The grey cloud**

A Find the words in the story. Read and complete.

1 This means NOT 'exciting'. ──→ (Page 52)

The trip was _b o r i n g_.

2 I'm more ill today than yesterday. ──→ (Page 52)

I'm _ _ _ _ _ today.

3 Water fell from my eyes. ──→ (Page 52)

I _ _ _ _ _ _ .

4 The cloud looked different. ──→ (Page 53)

It _ _ _ _ _ _ _ from white to grey.

5 You can skate on this. ──→ (Page 53)

There's _ _ _ on the ground.

6 This means NOT 'strong'. ──→ (Page 54)

I'm _ _ _ _ .

B Read and circle the correct answer.

1 When the cloud felt (frightened) / fine, it got colder.

2 Walking on ice is sometimes **safe** / **dangerous**.

3 On **Tuesday** / **Thursday**, Lily went to talk to the cloud.

4 Lily skipped along her **balcony** / **roof garden**.

5 It started to **rain** / **snow** when Lily talked to the cloud.

6 When Lily danced on the roof, she was on a **table** / **rock**.

C What is the happiest answer? Tick (✔) the correct answer.

A I'm all right. Don't feel bad. ☐

B I'm much better now, thanks. ☐

C I'm feeling worse today. ☐

D Choose and write *bad*, *worse* or *worst*.

1 A .... B .... C ....

2 A .... B .... C ....

3 A .... B .... C ....

4 A .... B .... C ....

E Listen and write.

22

1 Age: ....10............

2 Favourite hobby: listening to ....

3 Favourite food: .... cake

4 Her best holiday place: in the ....

5 Worst weather: when it is ....

6 Best friend's name: ....

F Look at the pictures and read the story. Write 1, 2 or 3 words to complete the sentences.

Charlie and Pat's sad day

Pat and Charlie lived in a village and were very good friends. But last Saturday, Pat called Charlie on the phone and said, 'Dad's got to work in the city and we've got to move there. I'm really sad. I don't want to go …' Charlie wanted to help Pat. He thought quickly. He knew there were lots of exciting things to do in the city.

Examples

Pat and Charlie's homes were in ....*a village*........ .

Last ....*Saturday*........ , Pat phoned Charlie.

1 Pat was sad because his family had to move to ....

2 Charlie thought quickly because he wanted .... his friend.

'You can go to the cinema every week! Who's your favourite film star?' he asked. 'Jim Lift! He's really cool,' said Pat. 'Yes! He's fantastic,' said Charlie. 'And sometimes there are funfairs. Famous pop stars sing in the park there, too.' 'Like Daisy Day!' said Pat. 'Yes!' said Charlie. 'And you love swimming and skating! There's a huge pool in the city and when everything gets really cold, you can go ice skating on the river there.'

'You're right, Charlie,' Pat said. 'I'm happier now.'

'Good!' said Charlie. 'I shall send you a funny text every evening. See you!'

3 In the city, Pat can go to the cinema and see Daisy Day in the .... too!

4 Pat can do his favourite sports in the .... and on the river.

5 Charlie says he can send Pat .... every day.

Charlie went to find his mum because he was really sad that Pat had to move. 'But I didn't want him to know that,' Charlie said. 'You're a good friend,' Mum said. 'Are you hungry? Let's make your favourite chocolate pancakes!'

6 Charlie wanted to talk to .... because he was sad.

7 Mum wants to make some .... for Charlie.

G

Look and read and write.

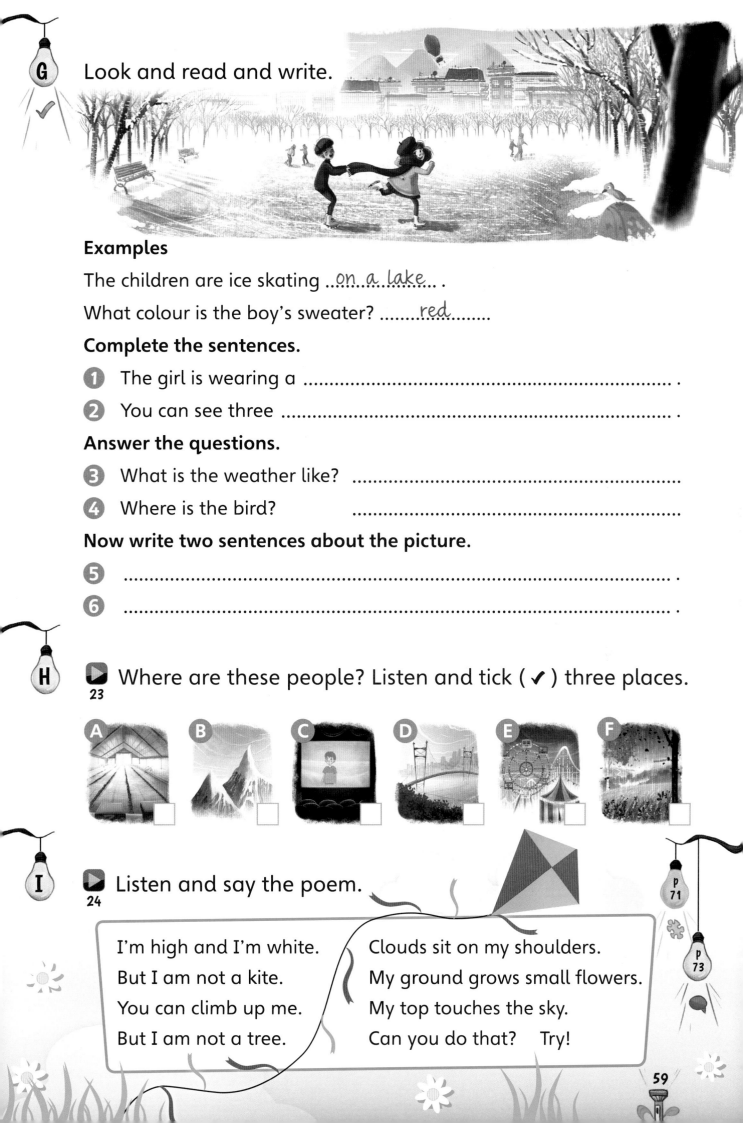

Examples

The children are ice skating ...on a lake... .

What colour is the boy's sweater? ....red........

Complete the sentences.

1. The girl is wearing a ....

2. You can see three ....

Answer the questions.

3. What is the weather like? ....

4. Where is the bird? ....

Now write two sentences about the picture.

5. ....

6. ....

H

23 Where are these people? Listen and tick (✔) three places.

| A | B | C | D | E | F |

I

24 Listen and say the poem.

I'm high and I'm white.

But I am not a kite.

You can climb up me.

But I am not a tree.

Clouds sit on my shoulders.

My ground grows small flowers.

My top touches the sky.

Can you do that?   Try!

p 71

p 73

The fancy-dress shop

Last Tuesday, Jim sent Zoe a text message about his party. It said:

ZOE ⚡ 13.45 🔋 97%

Hi Zoe, I'd like to invite you to my birthday party on Thursday at three o'clock. The address is 31, Lake Road. Wear fancy dress! See you on Thursday, Jim!

'Great!' thought Zoe. 'Parties are always fun, but a fancy-dress party is very exciting!' She went to tell her mother about Jim's text.

'It's fun to dress up,' said Zoe. 'I haven't got any fancy-dress clothes.'

'Well,' her mum answered, 'we can go to the new fancy-dress shop in the town centre. They've got lots of exciting things to wear there.'

So after lunch, Zoe's mother drove her to the fancy-dress shop in Duck Street!

When Zoe walked into the shop, she laughed! 'There are hundreds of things that I can wear here! Look, Mum! A firefighter's jacket and helmet, a fantastic snowman's costume, a nurse's uniform, a circus clown's trousers, a really cool panda costume! I can't choose!'

'How about this pineapple costume?' Zoe's mother said. 'Oh look! These kangaroo and kitten costumes are brilliant, too!'

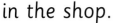

'Ermm ... no. I don't want any of those.'

'Then what about this doctor's coat?' Zoe's mother asked.

'Ermm ... no.' But then Zoe saw a pirate's costume. She loved it.

'That's the best one! Can I try it, please?' she asked the man in the shop.

'Yes! You need a moustache and a beard for that costume, too. Here! Put them on,' he said, and gave her a curly moustache and a long black beard. 'There's a room at the back of the shop with a big mirror in it.'

Zoe carried the clothes and the beard and the moustache to the small room at the back of the shop and put on the trousers, boots, shirt, scarf and hat. Then she put on the moustache and beard. She smiled at her face in the mirror. 'I love this!' she thought. 'Yes. This is great. I'd like to be a pirate for one afternoon.'

Suddenly, Zoe felt the wind in her face. She looked down at her feet. They weren't on the floor of the small room at the back of the fancy-dress shop in Duck Street. She was on a big ship in the sea. Pirates ran up and down the ship. They all looked very busy.

'Come on!' one of the pirates shouted at her. 'We want some more treasure. Quick! Climb that sail and look for ships!'

But Zoe couldn't move! 'Am I dreaming?' she thought.

'What's the matter?' the angry pirate said. 'You aren't afraid of climbing the sails, are you?'
'Yes, I am!' Zoe answered.
'Then jump into the sea with the sharks!' he shouted. 'We don't want any frightened pirates on this ship!'
'This is getting scary! Where am I?' Zoe thought.

But then the pirate stopped shouting and looked at her carefully. 'I don't know you. Where did you come from? Did you come from another pirate ship?' he asked.

'No. I came from the fancy-dress shop in Duck Street,' Zoe said quietly. 'And I'd like to go back there now, please. I don't want to be a pirate for an afternoon.'

Then a huge wave splashed her face and hair. Water dripped off the end of her nose and off her moustache and beard. Her pirate hat, shirt and scarf got very wet, too.

She looked down at her feet again, but she didn't see the ship. She saw the floor of the shop. 'Mum!' she called. 'Come here quickly!'

What's the matter, Zoe?   'How did your face and all your pirate clothes get wet?' her mother asked.

'Don't ask me, Mum. I don't know!' Zoe said. 'But I know I don't want to wear this pirate costume again. Please give it back to the man.'

'All right. Would you like to change it for the alien costume?'

'No, Mum!' Zoe said and laughed. 'I don't want to go to the moon! Can I put on the kitten costume, please? Then children can come and play with me in our garden!'

The fancy-dress shop

8

A Find the words in the story and complete the sentences.

1. A huge w a v e made Zoe's hair wet.
2. Zoe wore a curly m _ _ _ _ _ _ _ _ on her face.
3. Pirates in stories like looking for t _ _ _ _ _ _ _ .
4. Some people have to wear a h _ _ _ _ _ on their head at work.
5. You can send a m _ _ _ _ _ _ to your friends with apps or on your phone or laptop.

B Who said this? Read and write A, B or C.

A

B

C

1. It's fun to dress up. ...A...

2. I'd like to be a pirate for one afternoon. ....

3. Where did you come from? ....

4. We can go to the new fancy-dress shop in the town centre. ....

5. Climb that sail and look for ships. ....

6. I don't want to go to the moon! ....

7. How about this pineapple costume? ....

C What's the matter? Ask and answer with a friend.

afraid, all right, angry, bad, **better,** brave, cold, **frightened,** good, hot, hungry, **OK,** sad, **sorry,** surprised, terrible, tired, **weak**

Are you frightened?

Yes!

D 26 Who was in town yesterday? Write these names around the picture on page 60. Then listen and draw lines.

Paul   Clare   Peter   Mary   Vicky   Lily   Jim

E What do these people look like? Look, read and write.

☐ ☐ ☐ ☐ 1 ☐ ☐

1 This kind of fruit has sweet juice inside.   ......*a pineapple*......

2 This animal often has black circles around its eyes.   ....

3 This person has a big smile and works in a circus.   ....

4 This is a really young, little cat.   ....

5 This person can help people who are sick in hospital.   ....

6 This animal has a long tail and can hop very quickly.   ....

F Which costume does Zoe want to try on? Read and complete the sentence.

'**How about** this whale costume, Zoe?'
'No, thanks! I don't like that one.'
'Well **what about** this alien costume?'
'No, I don't want to wear that!'
'**How about** this then, Zoe? It's a
...........................'s costume!'
'Yes! That's really cool! Can I try it on?'

G Read the text. Choose the right words and write them on the lines.

Pirates			
Many children enjoy .....*reading*..... stories about pirates. Most pirates in happy stories and children's movies are funny.	read	reads	reading
1 .... not all pirates were really like that. One famous pirate,	Or	Because	But
2 .... was called *Blackbeard*, had four ships. Three hundred pirates	what	who	which
3 .... for him and he was really scary. Another pirate, *Long Ben*, sailed	work	worked	working
4 his ship .... the Red Sea. You can look for that on a map, and you can	above	after	around
5 learn .... about famous pirates on the internet.	both	more	any

H Let's talk about books. Ask and answer with a friend. Make a diagram.

> When do you read at home?

> What's the name of your favourite book?

> Who do you read with?

> Where do you put your books?

reads at the weekend

My friend Lucy

favourite book is Peter Pan

reads with brother

I What kind of work do they do? Find the six wrong sentences and write them in the correct places.

I wear really long boots or shoes.
Kids laugh a lot when they watch me.
I paint my face to do my job.
✗ ~~I travel around the world on a ship.~~
I work in different parts of a hospital.

....
....

I like looking for treasure.
Some people think I'm scary.
My pet parrot often sits on my shoulder.
I try to make people better again.
Come and see me at the circus.
<u>I travel around the world on a ship.</u>

....

I have to wear a uniform at work.
I work with people who are ill in bed.
Doctors sometimes ask me to help them.
In some stories, I've only got one leg!
People have to buy a ticket to watch me.

....
....

J ▶ Listen and write. Who is Zoe talking to?
27

1	Name:	....
2	Doesn't work on:	....
3	Wears:	a ....
4	Plays:	.... at work
5	Works at:	the ....

I'm talking to
....

p 71

p 73

Let's have fun!

1 Make puppets and act out a story.

You can have these ice skates. Would you like them?

Yes, please. I'd like your ice skates.

2 Plan a picnic and make a poster.

SCHOOL PICNIC

At 3.30 pm

In Class 2A

Bring some food and drink

3 Draw and talk about mountains.

The sun is above me.
A bear lives in my cave.

4 Design a computer game. What must players do?
Tell your classmates.

You must click
the mouse to ...

click the mouse to ...

press enter to ...

to pause game, press ...

press ... to quit game

move the ... with the
arrow keys

5 Design a farm.

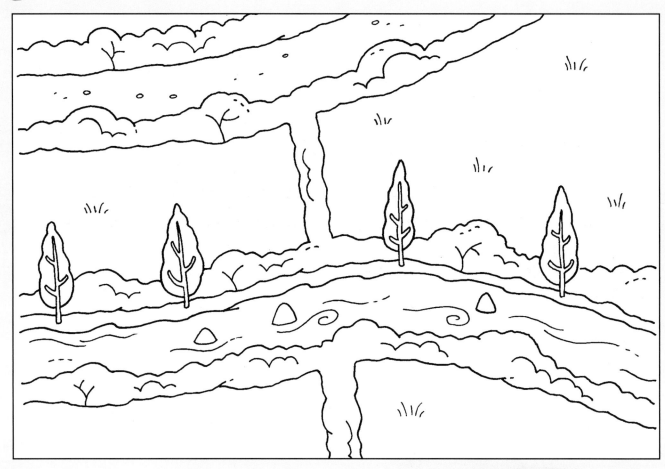

6 Write questions for an animal quiz.

1 What is the biggest animal in the world?   Blue whale.

2 ....

3 ....

4 ....

5 ....

7 Make a cloud information mobile.

Cirrus: really high and can bring ....snow........

Cumulonimbus: grey clouds that we can see before scary ....

Nimbostratus: grey clouds that we can see when it's ....

Cumulus: round on top and we see these in warm, ... weather

Stratus: low in the sky and can look like ....

snow   raining   sunny   storms   fog

8 Draw a fancy dress costume and complete the text.

Come to our party on Sunday! Wear a funny costume and bring some of your favourite food.

✉ ✶ 11.47 🔋 67%

Thanks for the invitation Lucy! I've got a .... costume I can wear. I love eating .... and I can bring that! I can bring my .... too. See you :)

Let's speak!

1 **What do you like to do? Where? Ask and answer.**

What do you like doing?

I like reading.

Where do you like doing that?

In the park.

2 **What can you see in the countryside? Listen to your friend and draw.**

I can see a river.

3 **Play the game. Make and say funny sentences.**

A man is older than a boy.

A computer game is more exciting than a CD.

4 **What can we do? Talk to your friend.**

This is boring. I like being busy. What can we do now?

How about playing a computer game?

5 What would you like to do on Saturday? Talk to your friend.

6 What's the matter? Ask and answer.

7 Make a friend happier. Write a conversation and act it out.

8 What can you wear? Ask and answer.

Let's say!

1
28

A white swan always takes Jane's wheel when she washes her bike with water.

2
29

Sue and Grace are cycling in circles in the sun.

3
30

Daisy and the kind tiger rode their bikes at night with green lights.

4
31

Mark carried tomatoes and helped his parrot make tomato sauce.

▶ **5**
32
Tom and a goat ate cold tomango soup on a boat.

▶ **6**
33
Fred played a board game with a dangerous whale on his birthday.

▶ **7**
34
Lily and the cloud grew flowers around the town.

▶ **8**
35
Robert dressed as a pirate with a curly moustache at the circus.

Wordlist

1 Jane's clever idea

nouns
afternoon
animal
bag
band
beach
bear
bed
bedroom
bee
Ben
bike
birthday
boot
bottle
butterfly
car
CD
Clare
cousin
daughter
duck
everyone
farm
father
field
football
forest
Friday
friend
funfair
girl
granddaughter
grandmother
grandparent
grandson
grass
ground

head
helmet
hobby
home
house
ice skates
idea
Jane
kitchen
lake
laptop
lemonade
Lily
map
Matt
Miss
moon
mother
Mr
mum
music
one
pair
park
part
path
Paul
people
rabbit
river
road
room
Sam
school
seat
sister
skateboard
snail
something
son

song
swimming
swimsuit
tennis racket
thing
town
two
uncle
walk
website
wheel

adjectives
boring
clever
cool
different
dirty
exciting
fantastic
fine
great
happy
last
new
nice
OK
old
right
round
short
slow
small

verbs
answer
ask
be
build
buy
call
can

do
fall
find
fix
get
give
go
have
hop
know
laugh
learn
let
like
listen
live
look
love
make
mean
need
play
rain
ride
say
see
sing
stand
start
stop
swim
talk
take
tell
think
try
walk
want
wash
wear

adverbs
always
back
down
inside
more
most
never
now
outside
quickly
really
upstairs
very
prepositions
around
before
behind
between
from
inside
near
opposite
under
expressions
oh dear
please
sorry
thanks

② The perfect present

nouns
alphabet
apple
aunt
back
banana
basketball
bean
bee
boat
bookcase
bowl
break
butterfly
cheese
child
circle

classmate
classroom
clock
countryside
cow
door
earache
email
family
fly
flower
food
frog
garden
gold
Grace
grape
grass
grown-up
home
homework
idea
internet
Jim
Julia
leaf
lemon
lime
lizard
milk
mistake
morning
parent
pea
pen
Peter
picnic
place
plant
playground
present
river
rock
salad
sand
sandwich
Saturday
sea

shape
shell
ship
sky
snail
sun
teacher
train
trip
vegetable
watch
water
weather
website
weekend
word
work
world
adjectives
angry
beautiful
blue
brilliant
cloudy
difficult
fat
favourite
funny
green
perfect
pretty
quiet
sunny
white
yellow
verbs
catch
choose
climb
cook
eat
fish
fly
grow
help
jump
move
paint

send
sit
sleep
stop
take
teach
watch
write
adverbs
slowly
sometimes
prepositions
above
along
expressions
all right

③ Daisy's tiger dream

nouns
balcony
bird
boat
book
breakfast
cat
cave
clothes
comic
computer
crayon
dad
Daisy
day
dinner
downstairs
dream
dress
face
game
guitar
hundred
Jack
jacket
kitten
lesson
light
mouth

movie
night
orange
paint
phone
question
roller skates
sailing
Sally
star
step
tiger
today
TV
wind
window
adjectives
big
black
brave
frightened
funny
good
kind
little
loud
strange
young
verbs
come
count
enjoy
hear
meet
open
phone
pick
point
sail
sleep
smile
speak
understand
adverbs
again
loudly
quietly

④ A busy Monday
nouns
Alex
answer
basement
bathroom
boat
boy
bread
bus
café
cage
centre
Charlie
cinema
circus
coffee
cook *
cup
dentist
door
e-book
evening
everything
film
floor
game
goal
grandpa
hall
hand
helicopter
hockey
instruction
Jack
Julia
kangaroo
library
lion
lunch
man
Mark
market
meat
message
mirror
model
Monday

noodles
onion
panda
parrot
person
pet
piano
pie
piece
plant
pool
potato
practice
puppy
radio
rug
sauce
snow
soup
spaceship
sport
square
street
supermarket
sweater
table
text
tomato
truck
video
wall
washing
machine
week
zebra
adjectives
asleep
awake
busy
dangerous
deep
easy
hot
open
quick
safe
square
sweet
terrible

tidy
verbs
carry
catch
clean
close
dream
drive
dry
email
help
hop
let
mean
practise
read
score
send
teach
video
wash
water
work
worry
expressions
hooray
oh dear

⑤ The tomango tree
nouns
banana
bat
building
bus
cake
chicken
city
country
cow
DVD
fishing
fruit
goat
hill
jungle
kiwi
mango
mountain
name

pear
photo
pineapple
plant
sheep
story
teacher
tomato
tractor
tree
waterfall
watermelon
adjectives
big
brown
cold
hungry
lucky
red
tall
wonderful
verbs
dance
kick
plant
put
read
sail
show
travel
adverbs
carefully
soon
suddenly
prepositions
below

6 **Do whales have stomach-ache?**

nouns
address
age
apartment
arm
armchair
ball
body
brother
chair

cough
dalmatian
doctor
dog
doll
dolphin
drink
ear
eye
Fred
glass
headache
heart
jeans
jellyfish
juice
leg
medicine
mouth
octopus
pancake
penguin
picture
polar bear
poster
rainbow
shark
shoulder
shower
spoon
spot
stomach
stomach-ache
tail
temperature
time
tooth
toothache
whale
woman
zoo
adjectives
bad
big
horrible
ill
interesting
scary
silly

strong
ugly
verbs
bounce
hurt
run
skateboard

7 **The grey cloud**

nouns
chocolate
cloud
coat
colour
dance
foot
holiday
ice
lift
kite
nothing
pop music
roof
station
Thursday
Tuesday
village
Wednesday
year
yesterday
adjectives
famous
grey
high
huge
long
sad
top
weak
wet
verbs
appear
change
cry
feel
frighten
skate
skip
touch

wave
adverbs
often
only

8 **The fancy-dress shop**

nouns
alien
app
beard
cat
costume
fancy-dress
firefighter
hair
hat
hospital
job
kid
Mary
moustache
nose
nurse
party
pirate
scarf
shirt
shoe
snowman
ticket
treasure
trousers
uniform
Vicky
Zoe
adjectives
afraid
curly
sick
sorry
tired
verbs
dream
invite
send
shout
splash
surprise

Acknowledgements

The author would like to acknowledge the shared professionalism and FUN she's experienced whilst working with colleagues during 20 years of production of YLE tests. She would also like to thank CUP for their support in the writing of this second edition of Storyfun.

On a personal note, Karen fondly thanks her inspirational story-telling grandfather, and now, three generations later, her sons, Tom and Will, for adding so much creative fun to our continuation of the family story-telling and story-making tradition.

The author and publishers would like to thank the following ELT professionals who commented on the material at different stages of development: Michelle and Silvia Ahmet Caldelas (Spain); An Nguyen (Vietnam); Alice Soydas (Turkey); Sarah Walker (Spain).

Design and typeset by Wild Apple Design.

Cover design and header artwork by Nicholas Jackson (Astound).

Audio production by Hart McLeod, Cambridge.

Music by Mark Fishlock and produced by Ian Harker. Recorded at The Soundhouse Studios, London. The authors and publishers acknowledge the following sources of copyright material and are grateful for the permissions granted. While every effort has been made, it has not always been possible to identify the sources of all the material used, or to trace all copyright holders. If any omissions are brought to our notice, we will be happy to include the appropriate acknowledgements on reprinting and in the next update to the digital edition, as applicable.

The authors are grateful to the following for permission to reproduce copyright photographs and material:

Key: B = Below, BL = Below Left, BR = Below Right, T = Top, TL = Top Left, TR = Top Right.

p. 68 (BR): Westend61/Getty Images; p. 69 (TR): M Nader/Stockbyte/Getty Images; p. 69 (BL): colematt/iStock/Getty Images Plus/Getty Images; p. 72 (TL): Kali Nine LLC/E+/Getty Images; p. 72 (TR): SerrNovik/iStock/Getty Images Plus/Getty Images; p. 72 (BL): Tony Garcia/Image Source/Getty Images; p. 72 (BR): skynesher/iStock/Getty Images Plus/Getty Images; p. 73 (TL): Caiaimage/Sam Edwards/OJO+/Getty Images; p. 73 (BL): Peter Muller/Cultura/Getty Images.

The following photographs on pages p. 73 (TR), p. 73 (BR) were taken on commission by Stephen Bond Photography for Cambridge University Press.

The authors and publishers are grateful to the following illustrators:

Rosie Brooks (Beehive Illustration) pp. 48 (dentist, bottle, doctor), 75 (Image 6); Alan Brown (Advocate) pp. 28, 29, 30, 31, 32, 33, 34, 35, 75 (B); Chiara Buccheri (Lemonade) pp. 60, 61, 62, 63, 64, 65, 66, 67, 75 (Image 8); Ray and Corinne Burrows (Beehive Illustration) 74 (Image 3), 75 (T); Roland Dry (Beehive Illustration) pp. 36, 37, 38, 39, 40, 41, 42, 43; Chiara Fedele (Astound) pp. 4, 5, 6, 7, 8, 9, 10, 11, 68 (T), 74 (T) Mandy Field (Phosphor Art) pp. 20, 21, 22, 23, 24, 25, 26, 27; Gustavo Mazali (Beehive Illustration) pp. 69 (T), 71 (T); Javier Montiel pp. 12, 13, 14, 15, 16, 17, 18, 19, 74 (Image 2); Bill Piggins pp. 44, 45, 46, 47, 48, 49, 50, 51, 70 (B); Alessia Trunfio (Astound) pp. 52, 53, 54, 55, 56, 57, 58, 59, 75 (Image 7).